INTERMEDIATE TO ADVANCED LEVEL

THE G. SCHIRMER INSTRUM Y



# THE TRUMPET COLLECTION

9 PIECES
BY 8 COMPOSERS

WITH TWO COMPANION CDS

ISBN: 978-1-4234-0667-9



G. SCHIRMER, *Inc.*

DISTRIBUTED BY
HAL•LEONARD® CORPORATION
7777 W. BLUEMOUND RD. P.O. BOX 13819 MILWAUKEE, WI 53213

**www.schirmer.com**
**www.halleonard.com**

# CONTENTS

# ABOUT THE MUSIC

## HERBERT L. CLARKE

American composer. Born in Woburn, Massachusetts, September 12, 1867.
Died in Long Beach, California, January 30, 1945.

**The Maid of the Mist**

Herbert Clarke is remembered primarily as a cornet player and band master. He was the soloist on cornet and assistant director of the famous "Sousa's Band," played trumpet in the New York Philharmonic, and played at the Metropolitan Opera. In his later life he served as band master in Ontario and California. Apart from his performing reputation, Clarke also invented new cornet models, wrote several method books on breath control and tonguing, and taught regularly. His compositions are largely for solo wind instruments, especially the cornet. The *Bride of the Waves* and *The Maid of the Mist* are examples of light classical material Clarke composed for soloist and band. On the recording, Mr. Niehaus performs this piece on a coronet.

## GEORGE ENESCU

Romanian composer. Born in Liveni Vîrna, August 19, 1881.
Died in Paris, May 3 or 4, 1955.

**Légende**
**for Trumpet and Piano**

A violinist from age 4, George Enescu (Georges Enesco in French) studied in Vienna and later at the Paris Conservatoire with Gabriel Fauré and Jules Massenet. After graduation, Enescu divided his time between Romania and Paris performing on the violin, conducting such ensembles as the Berlin Symphony Orchestra and the New York Philharmonic, and composing. Eternally dedicated to his homeland and its musical enrichment, Enescu founded the first Romanian opera company, introduced many Romanian folk songs into his music, and founded a competition to encourage young Romanian composers. Upon his death, his country honored him by renaming the region where the composer was born, George Enescu. *Légende* for Trumpet and Piano was composed in 1906 and dedicated to teacher, cornet player, and author of a cornet method book Merri Franquin (1848-1934).

## ALEXANDER GOEDICKE

Russian composer. Born in Moscow, March 4, 1877.
Died in Moscow, July 9, 1957.

**Concert Etude for Trumpet and Piano**
**in G minor, Op. 49**

Though a concert pianist, Goedicke also composed several orchestral pieces, four operas, and many smaller pieces. He studied piano at the Moscow Conservatory but received no formal training in composition. In 1900 he won the Rubenstein prize for Composition. Goedicke taught piano at the Moscow Conservatory and toured as a performer for many years. The Concert Etude is one of several pieces Goedicke composed for a solo brass instrument and orchestra, which included concertos for horn and trumpet. The composer later transcribed the Concert Etude for trumpet and piano.

## FRANZ JOSEPH HAYDN

German composer. Born in Rohrau, March 31, 1733.
Died in Vienna, May 31, 1809.

**Allegro**
**first movement from Trumpet Concerto in E-flat Major**

**Andante**
**second movement from Trumpet Concerto in E-flat Major**

One of the major composers of the eighteenth century, Haydn defined the sound of the classical style. He was employed by the Esterházy court for the majority of his career, serving two Princes from the Hungarian ruling family in Vienna as well as Hungary. Later in his life, Haydn spent time in London composing for the German violinist and musical impresario Johann Peter Salomon (1745-1815). Haydn lived the last years of his life in Vienna, composing large choral works. The Trumpet Concerto (Concerto per clarino) was commissioned by Anton Weidinger (1766-1852). Weidinger was an Austrian trumpet virtuoso. He began experimenting with the design of the trumpet, adding keys to expand the range from the natural harmonics. He succeeded, allowing the instrument a full diatonic spectrum. The concerto was completed in 1796, but not performed until 1800 as the new trumpet for which it was written was still being perfected. The new keyed trumpet was popular for a very short time, but it was quickly replaced by the modern valve trumpet. Trumpet player Mark Niehaus has composed a possible cadenza for this edition. On the recording, Mr. Niehaus performs the concerto on an E-flat trumpet.

## JOHANN NEPOMUK HUMMEL

Austrian composer. Born in Pressburg, November 14, 1778.
Died in Wiemar, October 17, 1837.

**Allegro con spirito**
**first movement from Trumpet Concerto in E-flat Major**

From the age of three, Johann Nepomuk Hummel showed remarkable intelligence and an interest in music. In the next few years he learned to play the violin and piano from his father. The family moved to Vienna where eight-year-old Johann studied with Mozart. The following year, Johann and his father decided to tour Europe, performing and teaching to great reception. The teenage Hummel curtailed his touring to study composition more seriously with Johann Albrechtsberger, Antonio Salieri, and Franz Joseph Haydn in Vienna. With these influential teachers, Hummel was able to develop connections in the musical world, including a dynamic relationship with Beethoven. Hummel became Konzertmesiter for Prince Nikolaus Esterházy at Eisenstadt, performing the duties of the now emeritus Kappelmeister Haydn. In 1811, Hummel was fired from this post and returned to Vienna. He married singer Elisabeth Röckel, who encouraged him to revive his touring career. Life on the road was not stable enough financially or emotionally for the Hummel's small children. Johann was able to secure a post in Stuttgart and finally became grand-ducal Kapellmeister at Weimar. From 1819 until his death, Hummel conducted, composed, and performed around Europe. His trumpet concerto, originally for the keyed trumpet, remains one of his works that is still performed. The work was composed in 1803 when Hummell was studying with Haydn and was never published. Though written in the key of E, the concerto is most often performed in E-flat. On the recording, Mr. Niehaus performs the concerto on an E-flat trumpet.

## JOHANN BAPTIST GEORG NERUDA

Czech composer. Born in Rosice, c. 1711.
Died in Dresden, October 11, 1776.

**Allegro**
**first movement from Concerto in E-flat Major for Trumpet and Strings**

Violinist, cellist, composer, and teacher, Neruda lived most of his life in Dresden where he was a violinist for Count Rutowski. Scholars estimate his birth in 1711 based on known dates that he served in the theatre orchestra in Prague. The majority of his works have been lost, but several symphonies, chamber pieces, and solo works remain extant. The concerto for the *corna da caccia* (natural trumpet) is Neruda's most famous work. As was common practice, the composer did not include a cadenza, assuming the performer would improvise an impressive passage demonstrating skill and understanding of the music. Trumpet player Mark Niehaus has composed a possible cadenza for this edition. On the recording, Mr. Niehaus performs the concerto on an E-flat trumpet.

## JOSEPH GUY ROPARTZ

French Composer. Born in Guingamp, June 15, 1864.
Died in Lanloup, November 22, 1955.

**Andante et Allegro**

Ropartz took an interest in music and poetry from a young age, encouraged by his parents. He matriculated at the Jesuit College in Vannes where he studied music and law. Ropartz continued his education at the Paris Conservatoire with Céasar Frank and Jules Massenet. At the age of thirty, he became the director of the conservatory in Nancy, and later director of the Strasbourg Conservatoire. In 1919 Ropartz retired from his academic career, moved back to the northern coast of France, and spent the next thirty-five years composing orchestral music, chamber pieces, an opera, incidental music for plays, and many smaller solo works. He also published several volumes of poetry.

## MAURICE C. WHITNEY

American Composer. Born in Glens Falls, NY, March, 25, 1909.
Died in Glens Falls, NY, September 2, 1984.

**Allegro scherzando**
**third movement from Concertino for Trumpet and Piano**

Maurice Whitney was a composer, arranger, conductor, educator, theorist, and performer who lived most of his life in upstate New York. He published many books and articles on church music and music education, had performances around the world by major orchestras and school bands, and published more than one hundred of his arrangements and original compositions for band, choir, orchestra, and smaller ensembles. Whitney was educated at Ithaca College, New York University, Columbia University, Westminster Choir College, and The New England Conservatory. Most of Whitney's work was composed for the schools and churches in which he worked. The Concertino for Trumpet and Band was transcribed by the composer for trumpet and piano and first published in 1959.

## A NOTE ON ARTICULATION AND PHRASING

Articulation and phrasing decisions are often left up to the performer or teacher, particularly in Baroque music, based on ability level, as well as interpretation. We have included minimal articulation and phrasing markings in the music, which should be treated as suggestions, and not necessarily the only solution for a given passage. The artist on the recording uses articulations and phrasings that do not always reflect the printed markings, but demonstrate his personal musical ideas for the repertoire. We encourage you to experiment with different approaches that convey the music for you and your abilities.

# The Maid of the Mist

Herbert L. Clarke
(1867–1945)

**Introduction**
**Tempo di Pollacca**

Andantino
12
p dolce
p
18
mf
mf
23
f
f
28
f

33
Tempo di Polka
mf
f
37
daintily
mf
41
46
faster
faster

50
Allegro
f
55
60
Trio
meno
p
meno
p
65
mf
mf

70
accel.
accel.
74
ff
ff
opt.
1.
rit.
rit.
2.
rit.
rit.
f
78
a tempo
a tempo
82

86
90
Coda
94
f
mf
98
mf

102
106
110
114
p

118
122
126
accel. e cresc.
f
f accel. e cresc.
130
ff
ff
ffz

# Légende

## for Trumpet and Piano

George Enescu
(1881–1955)

Expressif
Hésitant
En dehors
Pathétique
Cédez
Mouvt
Expressif
Cédez un peu
Gracieux
Très fondu
Ped.

22
Ped.
24
augmentez
Ped.
26
Animez
Cédez à volonté
Suivez
Ped.
28
Mouvt agité
Ped.

30
A volonté
31
Ier mouvt
Chantant
Augmentez
33
35
Facilité
A volonté
Suivez
m.d.

37
ff Très marqué
39 Pressez beaucoup
Vite
43 Très retenu
sff Sec
Vif (𝅗𝅥 = ♩)
f
sff
f
48
sf

51
A volonté
Mouvt
Suivez
Augmentez
56
59
62
Mettez la sourdine
Très long
8va
Fureusement
Très long

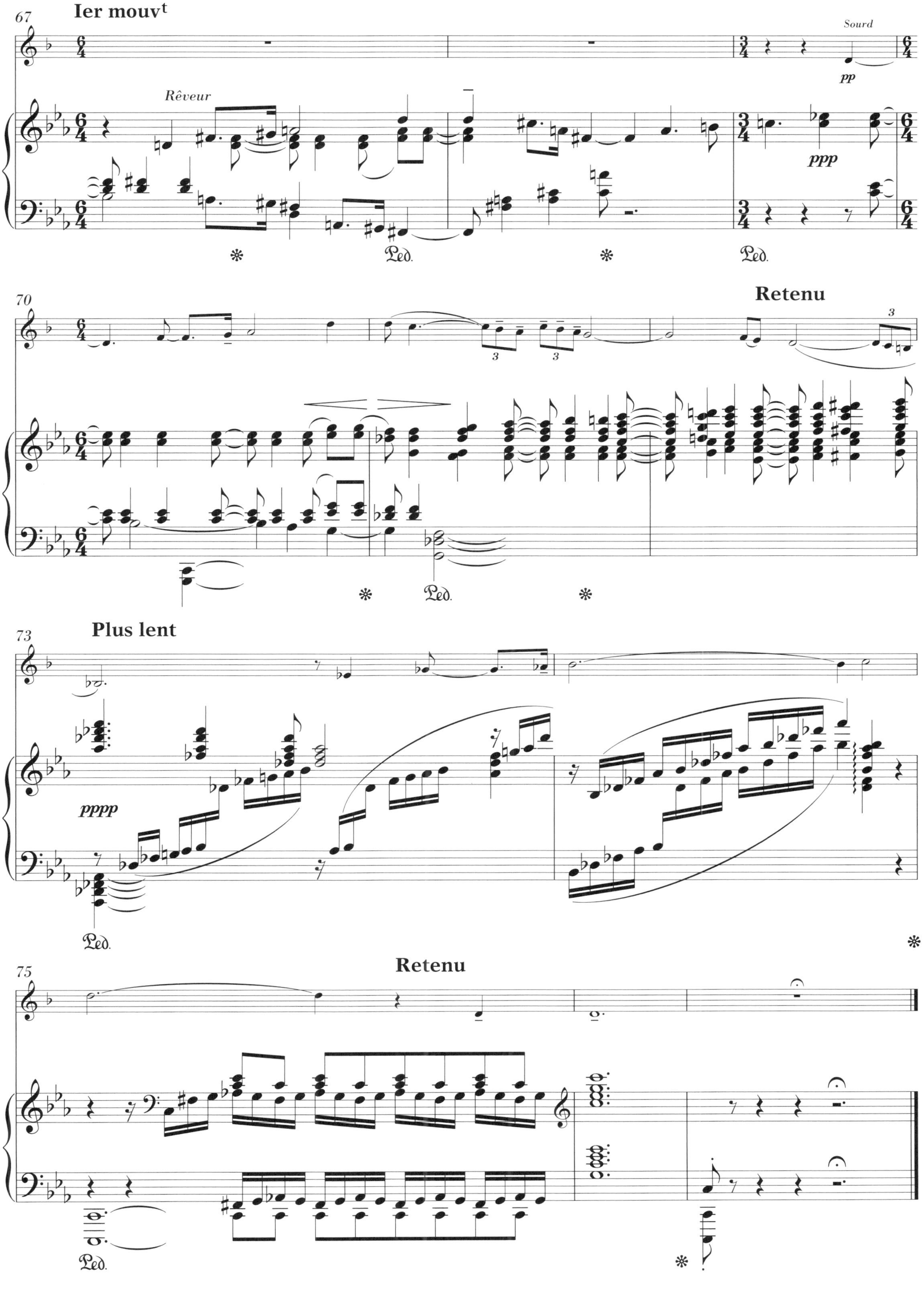
67
Ier mouvt
Rêveur
Sourd
pp
ppp
Ped.
70
Retenu
Ped.
73
Plus lent
pppp
Ped.
75
Retenu
Ped.

# Concert Etude for Trumpet and Piano

in G minor, Op. 49

Alexander Goedicke
(1877–1957)

**Allegro molto**

13
p
17
cresc.
f
21
p
simile
p
cresc.
24
cresc.
p
p
cresc.

28
f
f
ff
32
mf
ff
p
p
36
p
39
fp
fp
f

42
f
ff
45
mf
48
Quasi cantabile
f
f
53
p
p
cresc.
cresc.

58
mf
simile
p
p
62
f
fz
65
8va
ff
mf
68
cresc.

72
mf p
f p
p
76
p
p
80
p cresc.
p cresc.
mf
mf mf
simile
mf
f
83
f

86
ff
89
Quasi cantabile
f
ff
92
95

98
mf
ff
101
simile
p cresc.
p cresc.
104
cresc.
f
ff pesante
ff
rit.
rit.
108
tr
rall.
rall.
a tempo
ff p
a tempo
ff
p

112
dim.
dim.
116
mf
p
f
120
p
p
dim.
dim.
124
pp
p
pp

# Allegro

first movement from Trumpet Concerto in E-flat Major

Piano Reduction by Hansel Powell

Franz Joseph Haydn
(1733–1809)

*The trumpet notes in measures 8 and 13–16 are those played by the first trumpet in the orchestral version. The solo begins in measure 37.

16
p
20
24
f
27
30

34
f
p
38
43
tr
tr
f
p
f
47
p
f
mp
p
f

51
mf
p
55
f
p
60
tr
f
mf
64
mp dolce

68
f
p
73
p
cresc.
77
mf
f
p
f
p
f
f
p
82
tr
f

85
tr
88
p
93
mp
mf
f p
98
f
p
f
101
meno
dolce
p

104
107
110
mf
114
p

119
124
f
128
tr
tr
132
f
p
f
p

136
tr
f
f
p
140
mp
f
143
mf
p
f
147
f
p
f

151
tr
mp
p
154
f
p
157
p
cresc.
f
162
f

167
(rit.)
Cadenza
f
(rit.)
5
3
tr
mp
5
mf
ff
f
tr
tr
mf
f
170

# Andante

second movement from Trumpet Concerto in E-flat Major

Piano Reduction by Hansel Powell

Franz Joseph Haydn
(1733–1809)

34
38
fz
fz
fz
42
46
p
pp

# Allegro con spirito

## first movement from Trumpet Concerto in E-flat Major

Piano Reduction by Hansel Powell

Johann Nepomuk Hummel
(1778–1837)

16
19
p
22
f
24
27

30
sf
p
33
sf
p
36
cresc.
39
f
42
p
sfz
p

45
sfz
p
f p
49
f
53
56
–DE
59
sf

62
p
66
3
f
mf
mp
71
p dolce
p
75

79
tr
mf
83
mf
f
86
sf
mf
90
mp

94
3
cresc.
cresc.
98
3
f
102
106
f

109
mp dolce
p
112
cresc.
117
opt.
marc.
121
mp

125
130
mp
cresc.
cresc.
134
mf
poco cresc.
f
mf
138
p
p
mf

143
tr
cresc.
sf
p
cresc.
146
f
f
149
152
VI–
155

157
3
3
160
163
166
169
–DE
p
cresc.

172
mf
f
175
3
f
p
meno
180
mf
mp dolce
p
184

188
mp dolce
192
196
cresc.
200
mf
poco cresc.

204
207
rit.
210
a tempo
a tempo
215
dolce

218
222
225
228
f
f
p
mp dolce
cresc.

232
mf
p
236
mf
240
f
mp
244
opt.
mf
pp

247
f
250
sf
253
mp dolce
mp
f p
256
mf
mp

260
opt.
p
264
mp
p
268
mp
272

276
280
mp
f
mf
f
283
mp
f
mp
mp
f
286
ff
ff

288
mf
p
291
f
mf
p
p
mp
295
mf
297
tr
cresc.
cresc.

299
f
f
302
304
sf
306
sf
sf
308

# Allegro

first movement from Concerto in E-flat Major for Trumpet and Strings

Piano Reduction by Joshua Parman

Johann Baptist Georg Neruda
(1711–1776)

21
f
26
31
tr
fp
36
tr
f
tr

–DE

63
tr
p
p
68
mf
tr
f
cresc.
f
73
p
tr
f
p
cresc.
f
78

83
VI–
fp
cresc.
88
f
93
98
tr
p

–DE

124
129
134
139

144
VI–
149
p
cresc.
154
f
tr
159
p
f

165
–DE
171
f
mf
176
tr
181
mp
p
tr

186
tr
tr
191
196
tr
p
f
tr
201
f
fp
mf
p
f
f

206
tr
rit.
rit.
fp
cresc.
212
Cadenza ad libitum
Cadenza ad libitum
f

217
222

# Andante et Allegro

Joseph Guy-Ropartz
(1864–1955)

23
cresc.
27
A
f
f
32
dim.
p
p
ff
37
p espress.
p
p

43
pp
pp
49
Allegro
f
f
mf
54
59

64
69
ff
f
74
p
p
79
f

84
p
89
lightly
3
3
f
p cresc.
B
f
p cresc.
94
99

104
f
cresc.
f
cresc.
109
ff
ff
114
rall.
rall.
Andante (Tempo I)
ff
119
p espressivo
p

124
dim.
129
Allegro
f
f
134
139
p

144
p
149
cresc.
154
159
3
3
ff
ff

164
Slower - Broadly
ff
ff
169
175
rit.
rit.
Allegro
più f
più f
180
stringendo
stringendo
allargando
allargando

# Allegro scherzando

third movement from Concertino for Trumpet and Piano

Maurice C. Whitney
(1909–1984)

25
mp
31
mf
f
mp
p
37
f
mp
p
43
f

48
mf
mp
53
mf
mf
mp
59
mf
65

71
espr.
mp
77
cresc.
83
f
mp
p
89

95
3
3
3
3
p
101
mf
mp
cresc.
106
f
111

116
121
mf
127
mp espr.
p
135
3
3

142
mp
mp
149
mf
cresc.
mp
cresc.
155
mp
p
f
161

167
mp
172
mf
f
mp
p
178
f
mp
184
f

189
mf
mp
194
mf
r. h.
mp
200
206
mp
mp
cresc.

212
mp
ff
p
218
f
f
224
ff
ff
230
ff